MICHIGAN FROGS, TOADS, AND SALAMANDERS

A Field Guide and Pocket Reference

James H. Harding
and
J. Alan Holman

Michigan State University Museum

Photography by James H. Harding, except where otherwise credited.
Illustrations by W. James Hunter

FIRST EDITION 1992

MSU is an Affirmative-Action Equal-Opportunity Institution. Cooperative Extension Service programs and materials are open to all without regard to race, color, national origin, sex, handicap, age or religion.

Issued in furtherance of Cooperative Extension work in agriculture and home economics, acts of May 8, and June 30, 1914, in cooperation with the U.S. Department of Agriculture.
Gail Imig, director, Cooperative Extension Service. Michigan State University, E. Lansing, MI 48824.

TABLE OF CONTENTS

Michigan Frogs, Toads, and Salamanders

INTRODUCTION

Amphibians make up only about two and one-half percent of all living species of animals with backbones, but they are important members of wildlife communities in many parts of the world. Amphibians first appeared some 360 million years ago and were the first animals with backbones to adapt to living on land. Despite this bold move, they remain tied to water in many ways. Living amphibians include the frogs and toads, salamanders, and the legless, tropical caecilians.

The word "amphibian" comes from Greek roots that mean "double life," because most amphibians begin life as aquatic larvae with gills and eventually transform into animals capable of living on land. Amphibians typically have rather thin, moist, scaleless skins and do not have claws on their feet.

Twenty-three species of amphibians have been recorded in Michigan. Frogs and toads are most familiar as conspicuous vocal inhabitants of wetlands and woods. Salamanders are less well known, spending most of their lives beneath woodland soils or the waters of ponds and lakes.

This book is a nontechnical guide for anyone wanting to identify Michigan's frogs, toads, and salamanders and to discover some of their fascinating habits. General information on amphibian anatomy, fossil history, behavior, conservation, and captive care is also included. On page 11 is a glossary of selected words used in the text. On page 142 is a list of recommended references for those wanting additional information.

IDENTIFYING MICHIGAN AMPHIBIANS

To identify an adult frog, toad, or salamander, compare it with the photographs in the species accounts (pages 14-101). The text describes the size, shape, and coloration of each species, as well as other species that might be confused with it. It also notes each species' distribution, population status, and preferred habitat and provides information on habits and behavior. Once you have tentatively identified a specimen, check the range map to see if it occurs in the area where you found it. If not, you may have made a mistake. Occasionally amphibians are discovered in places where they were previously unknown. This is sometimes due to animals either accidentally or purposely being moved to new habitats by humans.

If you should find a frog, toad, or salamander outside of the range shown for that species (or a species not described in this book), take photographs of the specimen and note the location. Report your find to the authors or to the Michigan Department of Natural Resources. Your observations could be important!

Identifying frog tadpoles and salamander larvae is often difficult, even for experts, and a complete identification guide to amphibian larvae is beyond the scope of this book. However, the larval stages of some species are described in the text or illustrated in photographs. A process of elimination, based on habitat type and sightings of adult amphibians in the area, will allow a tentative identification of many tadpoles and salamander larvae found in Michigan. The references noted on page 142 may provide additional help.

ACKNOWLEDGMENTS

T he information in this book was obtained from many sources, including the authors' field notes and published information on Michigan amphibians. The books listed in "For More Information" (page 142) are recommended for readers wishing more information about amphibians.

The range maps are based on those in Conant and Collins (1991) but have been updated and modified on the basis of specimens in the Museum of Zoology, University of Michigan, and the Michigan State University Museum, as well as the authors' field notes. The maps are intended as a general guide to species distributions and not for establishing range extensions or corrections.

The authors are grateful to the photographers who generously donated photographs used in this book. Photographs not credited were taken by James H. Harding. Line illustrations on page 10 were drawn by W. James Hunter.

Many friends and colleagues assisted in the preparation of this book. Dr. Ned Fogle and Thomas Weise, of the Michigan Department of Natural Resources (DNR), supplied information on laws affecting amphibians in the state, and William Taft, also of the Michigan DNR, and Theresa Moran helped obtain photographic specimens. Peter Wilson and James Fowler provided valuable technical and field assistance.

The authors also thank members of the MSU Department of Outreach Communications for their skillful and enthusiastic efforts in producing this volume.

CHECKLIST OF MICHIGAN AMPHIBIANS

ORDER　**Anura (= Salientia)**　　　**[Frogs and Toads]**

IDENTIFYING CHARACTERISTICS

The following illustrations show a "typical" frog, toad, tadpole, salamander larva, and salamander. Parts of the body often used in identification are labeled.

Frog

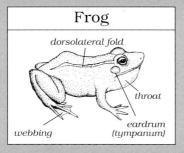

dorsolateral fold

throat

webbing

eardrum (tympanum)

Toad

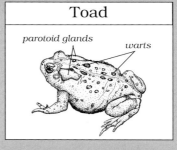

parotoid glands

warts

Tadpole

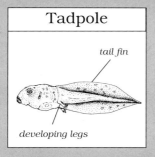

tail fin

developing legs

Salamander Larva

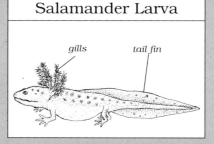

gills

tail fin

Salamander

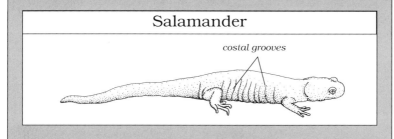

costal grooves

GLOSSARY
OF SELECTED TERMS

*N*ote: *The definitions below are based on the use of these terms in this book and may not include all possible meanings of these terms.*

Amplexus: A reproductive behavior in frogs and toads in which the male grasps the female's body from above with his forelegs. From this position the male fertilizes the eggs externally as they are laid.

Aquatic: Living in water.

Band: A marking or contrasting strip of color that goes across an animal's body from side to side.

Blotch: An irregular patch of color.

Carnivore: An animal that feeds on other animals.

Carrion: Dead animal matter.

Cloaca: An internal chamber in frogs and salamanders that receives both reproductive materials and body waste products and opens to the outside at the vent.

Dorsolateral fold: A ridge of skin along the sides of the back in some frogs.

Gelatinous: Jelly-like.

Herbivore: An animal that feeds on plants or plant products.

Hybrid: An animal or plant that results from the mating of two different species.

Intergrade: An animal that is intermediate between races or subspecies.

Invertebrate: An animal without a bony or cartilaginous skeleton, such as insects, spiders, worms, mollusks, etc.

Larva: The aquatic, gilled stage of an immature salamander or frog. (*Plural = Larvae.*) The larva of a frog or toad is called a tadpole.

Metamorphosis: The transformation of an amphibian from a larva to an adult.

Neotenic: A word that refers to an animal that can reproduce while still retaining larval features and habits.

Nocturnal: Active at night.

Omnivore: An animal that eats both animal and vegetable matter.

Parotoid glands: The large wart-like glands located behind each eye in toads and some salamanders.

Population: Members of a species of plant or animal living in a certain geographic area.

Predator: An animal that kills and eats other animals.

Relict population: A population of animals, isolated from the main range of its species, that has survived after the extinction of nearby populations of the same species.

Spermatophore: A cylindrical or cone-shaped gelatinous mass capped by sperm and deposited by male salamanders during or after courtship. The female takes the sperm into her cloaca to store for later fertilization of her eggs.

Stripe: A narrow marking or strip of color that usually occurs in the long dimension (head to tail) of an animal's body.

Tadpole: The aquatic larval stage of frogs and toads. (Sometimes called a polliwog.)

Tetraploid: A species that has twice the number of chromosomes as the species presumed to be its ancestor. (Chromosomes are structures which carry hereditary material in the body cells.)

Terrestrial: Living on land.

Trill: A type of frog call in which a series of notes is repeated very rapidly.

Tympanum: The rounded eardrum visible behind the eye of most frogs and toads.

Vent: The external opening of the cloaca through which amphibians expel body wastes and reproductive materials (eggs or sperm).

Vernal pond: A pond that contains water in the spring but may become dry in the summer.

Vertebrate: An animal with backbones and (usually) a bony skeleton.

MUDPUPPY

Necturus maculosus maculosus

DESCRIPTION:

A mudpuppy is a large, permanently aquatic salamander with bushy, reddish gills visible behind the head. Its body, sides, and tail are usually brown or grayish brown with scattered dark spots or blotches. The belly is grayish or yellowish and may also be spotted. The head is flattened and is broader behind the tiny, lidless eyes. There are four toes on each foot. Larval mudpuppies have a yellowish stripe down each side of the back. Mudpuppies have very slimy skins and are difficult to hold in the hand.

Adult length: 8 to 15 inches (20 to 38 cm); the record length is 19.13 inches (48.6 cm).

SIMILAR SPECIES:

Mudpuppies are neotenic, retaining larval features, such as external gills and tail fins, into adulthood. Small mudpuppies might be confused with the larval stages of other large salamanders, especially the tiger salamander (page 38). However, mudpuppies have four toes on the hind feet while all other potentially confusing

Adult

Adult – note external gills.

R.W. VanDevender

15

Michigan species have five toes on the hind feet. Sirens (page 18) are similar but are more eel-like and lack hind legs.

DISTRIBUTION AND STATUS:

Mudpuppies are found throughout Michigan. They are common in some places, but there are reports that the species has declined in portions of the Great Lakes and elsewhere. Mudpuppies are sensitive to chemicals used in fish management, such as rotenone and lampricides. They are undoubtedly affected by many water pollutants and should be considered for study by those involved in fisheries and water quality research.

HABITAT AND HABITS:

These salamanders inhabit rivers and lakes, including bays and shallows of the Great Lakes. They spend most of their time crawling on the bottom or hiding under objects in shallow water, but they have been reported at depths of nearly a hundred feet (30 meters). Mudpuppies are usually nocturnal in summer but will feed during the day, particularly if the water is cloudy or weedy. They are active throughout the year and are frequently caught in winter by people ice fishing.

Male and female mudpuppies congregate in shallow water in October and November for mating, but egg laying does not occur until the following spring. Females excavate a nest cavity under a submerged rock or other flat object. From 50 to 100 or more pea-sized eggs are suspended from the upper surface of the cavity, each hanging from a thin gelatinous stalk. The female stays with the eggs until the larvae hatch, which may take from one to two months. The larvae measure from .75 to 1.4 inches (2 to 3.5 cm) long at hatching and reach maturity in four to six years. Mudpuppies may live for more than 20 years.

Mudpuppies feed on a variety of small aquatic animals, including crayfish, snails, insect larvae, worms, and fish. Although they will eat fish eggs, there is no evidence that they damage natural fish populations.

Perhaps because of their strange appearance and slimy skins, mudpuppies are often destroyed by people who catch them on fish lines or in minnow traps. However, these salamanders are harmless to humans and human interests, and persecution is unwarranted.

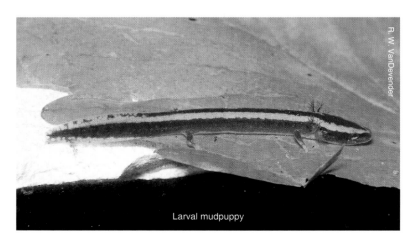

Larval mudpuppy

WESTERN LESSER SIREN

Siren intermedia nettingi

DESCRIPTION:

The lesser siren is an aquatic, eel-like salamander with small front legs and no hind legs. Bushy, reddish gills are visible behind the head. The color above varies from dark gray to brown or olive, often with scattered dark spots, and the belly is grayish with some light spotting. Very young larvae have bright orange markings on the head, a light stripe on each side of the body, and a fin along the top of the tail.

Adult length: 7 to 16 inches (18 to 40.6 cm); the record is 19.75 inches (50 cm).

SIMILAR SPECIES:

Mudpuppies (page 14) have four legs, while sirens (lacking hind limbs) have only two.

DISTRIBUTION AND STATUS:

The lesser siren is known from only two sites in Michigan, in Allegan County and Van Buren County in the southwest-

WESTERN LESSER SIREN

Adult

R.W. VanDevender

R.W. VanDevender

Head and gills of a young siren.

ern Lower Peninsula. It is possible that the species was introduced into the state by humans, but a natural population exists in northern Indiana and it is equally likely that sirens moved into Michigan on their own. Field studies are needed to determine if this inconspicuous salamander still inhabits the state.

HABITAT AND HABITS:

Lesser sirens inhabit shallow, weedy ponds, lakes and lake inlets, ditches, and sluggish streams. They are largely nocturnal, spending daylight hours buried in bottom debris or concealed in aquatic vegetation. If their environment dries up, they can survive by entering crayfish burrows or by burrowing into the mud and forming a protective "cocoon" out of body secretions. They may also move overland.

In spring a female siren deposits about 200 eggs in a shallow depression in the bottom mud. The larvae are about .43 inch (1.1 cm) long at hatching and mature in two to three years.

Sirens eat insect larvae, crustaceans, worms, and small snails. Although salamanders are usually considered silent creatures, lesser sirens reportedly make several types of sounds. These include a clicking sound produced underwater and various whistles or yelping sounds given when disturbed or captured.

The head and gills of a lesser siren.

BLUE-SPOTTED SALAMANDER
Ambystoma laterale

DESCRIPTION:

Blue-spotted salamanders are mostly black or grayish black with numerous pale blue or turquoise spots and flecks on the sides, legs, and tail, and often extending onto the back. The belly may be lighter than the back and is also blue-spotted.

Adult length: 3.5 to 5.5 inches (8.9 to 14 cm).

SIMILAR SPECIES:

Newly transformed blue-spotted salamanders often have yellowish rather than blue spots and can be confused with small spotted salamanders (page 26). The latter usually have larger yellow flecks on the back and an unspotted brown or tan belly. Small-mouthed salamanders (page 34) have smaller heads, shorter snouts, and grayish white blotchy markings. Hybrid *Amby-stoma* salamanders occur in Michigan but are difficult to distinguish using visible markings. Most hybrid populations are probably the result of interbreeding between blue-spotted salamanders

BLUE-SPOTTED SALAMANDER

R.W. VanDevender

Larva

R.W. VanDevender

Adult

R.W. VanDevender

Hybrid salamander

and the Jefferson's salamander (*Ambystoma jefferso-nianum*) that occurs south of Michigan. Mixing of the populations may have occurred due to the advance of glacial ice over the Great Lakes area at least 20,000 years ago. Some hybrid specimens closely resemble the blue-spotted salamander, but others may be paler, less heavily spotted, or spotted with white instead of blue. Laboratory analysis of chromosomes and red blood cells is required to properly identify hybrids.

DISTRIBUTION AND STATUS:

Blue-spotted salamanders are found throughout Michigan. They are often common in suitable habitats.

HABITAT AND HABITS:

Blue-spotted salamanders prefer moist deciduous hardwood forests but may occur in rather dry, disturbed woods as well as swamp woodlands. Ponds that hold water well into the summer are essential for breeding. This species is often found beneath logs and other forest debris throughout the summer and fall.

Blue-spotted salamanders normally breed in March or early April when stimulated by warm rains. Some overwinter near breeding ponds, while others migrate into the ponds from nearby woodlands. Males usually arrive a day or two ahead of the females. During courtship, which occurs underwater, the male clasps the female just behind her forelegs with his front feet and rubs his chin on her head. This is accompanied by tail and body movements, and the paired salamanders may surface occasionally for air. Eventually the male releases the female and moves forward, depositing one or more spermatophores (jelly-like masses capped with sperm) on the pond bottom. The female picks up the sperm with her cloaca and stores it internally until the eggs are fertilized.

Egg laying occurs a day or two after mating. Blue-spotted salamanders lay their eggs in small gelatinous masses containing from one to a dozen or more eggs, usually attached to submerged sticks or other debris. A female may produce from 35 to over 500 eggs per year. The larvae hatch in three or four weeks at about .4 inch (1 cm) in length, and are brown with yellowish markings on the back. Older larvae are darker, often with black mottling on the tail fin. The few larvae that survive the many perils of pond life leave the water in mid- to late summer, at a length of about 1.2 inches (3 cm). They reach breeding age in about two years.

Blue-spotted salamanders eat small invertebrates such as insects, spiders, centipedes, slugs, and earthworms. The larvae are also carnivorous and feed mostly on aquatic invertebrates.

These salamanders deter predators by lashing their tails and producing a noxious, foul-tasting substance from glands at the base of the tail. The head may be tucked beneath the tail for further protection.

SPOTTED SALAMANDER

Ambystoma maculatum

DESCRIPTION:

Spotted salamanders are black or dark grayish brown with two irregular rows of rounded yellow spots running from the head onto the tail. Spots on the head may be orange. Occasional specimens have cream or tan spots, and rare individuals may be nearly spotless. The unspotted belly varies in color from slate gray to purplish brown.

Adult length: 5 to 9.75 inches (12.7 to 24.8 cm).

SIMILAR SPECIES:

The larger tiger salamander (page 38) has numerous irregularly shaped yellowish spots and blotches which extend onto the sides and belly. Newly transformed blue-spotted salamanders (page 22) may have small yellow spots on the sides and belly, while very small spotted salamanders usually have unspotted grayish or brownish bellies.

DISTRIBUTION AND STATUS:

Spotted salamanders occur throughout Michigan and can be locally

Adult

R.W. VanDevender

Hand-held egg mass.

Larva

R.W. VanDevender

27

common. Their numbers have reportedly declined in parts of the state in recent years. This species is less tolerant of habitat disturbance than its smaller relative, the blue-spotted salamander. Acidification of breeding ponds can inhibit the development of spotted salamander eggs and larvae; thus acid precipitation may threaten the species in some areas of Michigan.

HABITAT AND HABITS:

This species inhabits moist woodlands near vernal ponds. They avoid cutover forests and those subject to flooding. Spotted salamanders spend much of their time underground and are rarely seen after the spring breeding season.

Warm rains and thawing ground in March or early April can spur the migration of spotted salamanders to their breeding ponds. Each salamander may return to the same pond year after year. Courtship, which occurs mostly at night, is often a group affair, with males circling about in the shallow water nudging other salamanders with their snouts. Upon contacting a female, the male crawls under her chin and moves forward, seeking a suitable place to deposit one or more spermatophores. The female may follow the male, moving from side to side, until she contacts a spermatophore. She then lifts her tail and picks up the packet of sperm with her cloaca. Fertilization probably takes place during egg laying, which occurs several hours to two days after courtship and mating.

A female spotted salamander lays up to 250 eggs, either in one mass or several smaller ones. Each group of eggs, surrounded by its protective gelatinous covering, is usually attached to a submerged stick or plant stem. Spotted salamander egg masses are rather stiff and will often hold their shape when lifted from the water, unlike the more flimsy egg masses of related species. The egg masses often appear greenish because of the growth of green algae (a single-celled plant) in the egg membranes. This may be mutually beneficial, since the algae could provide the developing salamander embryos with additional oxygen while obtaining carbon dioxide needed for their growth.

The eggs hatch in three to five weeks into brownish larvae about one-half inch (1.3 cm) long. Metamorphosis to the land stage occurs in two to four months, though slower-growing larvae may not transform until the following spring (assuming the pond does not dry out). The young salamanders mature in about two years and may live 20 years or more.

Spotted salamanders are carnivorous, eating small insects, worms, slugs, snails, centipedes, and similar prey. The larvae mainly eat small aquatic invertebrates.

This species may wave or lash its tail if disturbed, like related salamanders in the *Ambystoma* group. A noxious substance is secreted from glands at the base of the tail and parotoid glands behind the eyes. This foul-tasting substance may deter many predators.

MARBLED SALAMANDER

Ambystoma opacum

DESCRIPTION:

Marbled salamanders are black with white or gray bands across the back and tail. The bands may widen and merge into an irregular stripe extending along the upper sides and onto the head. The belly is black or brownish black. Normally, adult males have white bands and females have grayish bands.

Adult length: 3.5 to 5 inches (9 to 12.7 cm).

SIMILAR SPECIES:

This stocky, boldly marked species is unlikely to be confused with other Michigan salamanders. The small-mouthed salamander (page 34) is slimmer and has light markings in the form of irregular, scattered flecks.

DISTRIBUTION AND STATUS:

The only reported localities for the marbled salamander in Michigan are in Berrien, Van Buren, and Allegan counties in the southwestern corner

MARBLED SALAMANDER

Adult

Larva

Female with eggs.

R.W. VanDevender

R.W. VanDevender

of the state. This species may have been introduced into Michigan by humans. However, an isolated population of marbled salamanders exists in northern Indiana, a few miles south of the state line, and it is possible that the Michigan specimens are a natural relict population. Field studies are needed to determine if marbled salamanders still live in the state. Marbled salamanders are currently listed as a threatened species by the Michigan Department of Natural Resources and are protected by state law.

HABITAT AND HABITS:

Marbled salamanders typically inhabit moist woodlands. They are rarely found aboveground and spend most of their time burrowed in soil, in rodent tunnels, or beneath logs, rocks, or leaf litter.

The marbled salamander is unusual in that it breeds in the fall. Courtship and mating is similar to that of the spotted salamander (page 26), but takes place on land. (Marbled salamanders reportedly drown if submerged in water.) A female deposits from 75 to 200 eggs in a shallow depression under leaf litter, a log, or other shelter. The site is usually in a dry pond bed that later fills with water during autumn rains. The female often stays with the eggs until the nest is covered by water and the larvae hatch.

Fall hatching probably gives the larvae a head start in the competition with species of salamanders that breed in spring.

Marbled salamander eggs can remain dry for some time and still develop, but those that freeze before the pond fills will die. The larvae undoubtedly perish if a pond freezes completely during the winter. These factors may limit the northward expansion of this species.

Larval marbled salamanders metamorphose and leave the ponds in late spring or early summer when they are about 2 inches (5 cm) long. Newly trans-formed individuals are brown or black with silver-gray dots over the head, back, and tail. One study found that less than five percent of young marbled salamanders survive their first year. They can breed in two years and may live up to nine years after maturing.

These salamanders feed on small invertebrates, such as insects, earthworms, slugs, and snails. The larvae mainly eat aquatic invertebrates (including mosquito larvae) but also eat smaller amphibian larvae.

A new metamorph of the marbled salamander.

SMALL-MOUTHED
SALAMANDER

Ambystoma texanum

DESCRIPTION:

Small-mouthed salamanders have proportionally small heads and very short, blunt snouts. They are normally black, gray, or grayish brown with an irregular pattern of gray blotches and flecks which is usually heaviest on the sides. The belly is dark brown or black, sometimes with light spots.

Adult length: 4.5 to 7 inches (11.4 to 17.8 cm).

SIMILAR SPECIES:

Blue-spotted salamanders (page 22) have longer snouts and bluish spotting on the back and sides. The small-mouthed salamander occasionally will breed with other *Ambystoma* salamanders, including the blue-spotted salamander. This results in hybrid specimens that can show a blending of characteristics of the two species.

DISTRIBUTION AND STATUS:

In Michigan the small-mouthed salamander is known only from the southeast corner of

SMALL-MOUTHED SALAMANDER

R.W. VanDevender

Adult

Adult

R.W. VanDevender

the Lower Peninsula where it is rare and restricted to a few scattered localities. The species is common in parts of Ohio and Indiana. The small-mouthed salamander is currently listed as an endangered species by the Michigan Department of Natural Resources and is protected by state law.

HABITAT AND HABITS:

Moist hardwood forests with vernal ponds are the preferred habitat for this species in Michigan. They often remain in lowland areas near the breeding ponds and spend much time underground in crayfish or rodent burrows or beneath decaying logs.

The courtship and mating habits of the small-mouthed salamander are very similar to those of the spotted salamander (page 26), and these species may share the same breeding ponds in late winter or early spring. Females produce from 300 to 700 eggs, laid in small, flimsy gelatinous masses attached to submerged twigs or plants. The larvae hatch in two to eight weeks (depending on water temperature) and may metamorphose into the terrestrial form two to three months later when they are about 2 inches (5 cm) long.

Small-mouthed salamanders eat worms, insects, and other small invertebrates. They produce a noxious substance from glands at the base of the tail which discourages some predators. When threatened, a salamander may curl its body and bring its head under its tail, which is waved or lashed at the enemy.

Hybrid salamander *Ambystoma laterale* x *texanum*.

EASTERN TIGER SALAMANDER

Ambystoma tigrinum tigrinum

DESCRIPTION:

Adult tiger salamanders are robust animals with large heads, broad, rounded snouts, and small eyes. The color is variable, but they are usually dark brown, olive gray, or black, with many yellow, olive, or tan spots, streaks, and blotches on the head, back, sides, and tail. The belly can be brownish, yellowish, or gray, also with spots or streaks. Larvae are yellowish green, olive, or gray, with dark spotting and a light belly. Some populations of tiger salamanders produce neotenic individuals which do not metamorphose but instead mature and reproduce in the gilled larval form. This is Michigan's largest terrestrial salamander.

Adult length: 7 to 9 inches (17.8 to 22.9 cm). Record: 13 inches (33 cm).

SIMILAR SPECIES:

The smaller spotted salamander (page 26) has two irregular rows of rounded yellow spots, mainly on the upper surfaces, and a plain gray or brown belly.

EASTERN TIGER SALAMANDER

Adult

R. W. VanDevender

A new metamorph.

Larva showing head and gills.

DISTRIBUTION AND STATUS:

The tiger salamander is found in the southern and north central portions of the Lower Peninsula, and in Alger County in the Upper Peninsula. It varies in abundance but is locally common in some places.

HABITAT AND HABITS:

Tiger salamanders live in a variety of habitats, including woodlands, fields, marshes, farmlands, suburban areas, or wherever suitable breeding ponds are available. They spend most of their time underground and will excavate their own burrows or use burrows dug by other animals. These salamanders are often seen aboveground in spring and early fall during rainy periods. They frequently become trapped in window wells, basements, and swimming pools during these movements.

Tiger salamanders breed in March or April in almost any fishless body of water, including woodland ponds, farm ponds, ditches, and marshes. They share breeding sites with other salamanders but tend to choose deeper water. Some individuals reportedly overwinter in or near the breeding ponds, while others migrate to the ponds when early spring rains thaw the ground. Courtship is similar to that of the spotted salamander (page 28) except that the male may shove a female away from other males by nudging her along, then walk under her chin to encourage her to follow him. The female nudges the male's tail, causing him to deposit a spermatophore.

She may then pick up the sperm with her cloaca for later fertilization of the eggs.

Each female lays from 100 to over 400 eggs in several loose, gelatinous masses attached to objects near the bottom of the pond. The incubation period depends on water temperature, but the larvae normally hatch in 20 to 30 days. They are only about .6 inch (1.5 cm) long at hatching, but they grow quickly and by mid- to late summer are ready to metamorphose to the terrestrial form at a length of 2.75 to 5.7 inches (7 to 14.5 cm). They mature in two to five years and may have a lifespan of 20 years or more. Many tiger salamander eggs and larvae are eaten by predators, and in drought years breeding ponds may dry up before any larvae reach metamorphosis.

Adults can defend themselves by secreting a noxious substance from glands on the tail; the tail may be lashed at an offender. Of the many tiger salamanders observed by the authors, however, none have attempted any defense other than walking away or trying to wiggle out of a restraining hand.

Insects, worms, slugs, and snails are eaten by adult tiger salamanders. Larvae eat aquatic invertebrates, tadpoles, and smaller salamander larvae.

EASTERN NEWT
Notophthalmus viridescens

DESCRIPTION:

Newts have an unusual life history that includes an aquatic larval stage, an intermediate land-living stage called the eft, and an aquatic adult stage. The adults are olive to brownish green above and yellow on the throat and belly, with small black dots scattered over much of the body. There are two sub-species in Michigan, the red-spotted newt and the central newt (note ranges below). The red-spotted newt (*Notophthalmus viridescens viridescens*) usually has two rows of black-bordered red spots down the back, while the central newt (*Notophthalmus viridescens louisianensis*) lacks the red spots, or the spots are smaller and only partly bordered by black. In the breeding season, adult male newts differ from females in having higher tail fins and black, thickened bumps on the rear legs and toes.

Adult length: 2.5 to 5.5 inches (6.4 to 14 cm).

Efts are red, orange, or rusty brown above and yellowish on the belly, and have a dryer, rougher skin texture than other salamanders. Those in the

42

Adult

R.W. VanDevender

Red Eft

Larva

43

process of changing to the adult form may be very dark in color.

Efts are from 1.4 to 3.4 inches (3.5 to 8.6 cm) long.

DISTRIBUTION AND STATUS:

Newts are found throughout Michigan. The red-spotted newt occurs in the southeastern counties of the Lower Peninsula, while the central newt occupies the rest of the state. Intergrade specimens may be found in the southern Lower Peninsula. Newts are common in some parts of Michigan but are scarce in many areas that seem to have suitable habitats.

HABITAT AND HABITS:

Adult newts inhabit ponds, marshes, and shallow lakes. They are most abundant in permanent, fishless ponds with ample growth of aquatic plants. In deeper ponds they can remain active throughout the year. Efts are usually found near breeding ponds, under logs, rocks, boards, and other objects, but they may be seen walking in the open during and after rainstorms. If a pond dries up, the adult newts can again become terrestrial, at which time their tail fins shrink and their skins darken and become rougher.

Breeding takes place from March to June. A courting male may clasp the female's neck with his hind legs and fan her with his tail, probably spreading an odorous substance that stimulates the female to breed. After additional fanning and nudging, the male moves forward and deposits a spermatophore; the female then moves over it and picks up the sperm with her cloaca. The eggs are fertilized internally.

Females may lay from 200 to over 300 eggs during a season. Each egg is enclosed in a gelatinous covering and is attached to an aquatic plant or other object. The tiny gilled larvae hatch in three to five weeks. They grow rapidly and most leave the pond in late summer as land-living efts. The eft stage can last from two to seven years. A second metamorphosis then occurs when the eft returns to the water and attains the form and coloration of an adult newt. In some areas the eft stage may be skipped, with the larvae transforming directly into aquatic adults.

Newts feed on small aquatic invertebrates, including mosquito larvae and pupae, as well as eggs and larvae of other amphibians. Efts eat insects, worms, and small snails.

Newts produce a poisonous secretion from skin glands that is harmful or distasteful to many predators. The bright color of the efts may warn potential enemies of their toxic nature.

RED-BACKED SALAMANDER

Plethodon cinereus

DESCRIPTION:

This is a thin little salamander with small legs and feet. There are two color phases. A "redback" phase salamander is black or gray with a reddish or orange stripe down the back, from the neck onto the tail. The "leadback" phase lacks the red stripe and is gray or black above, often with tiny, scattered white or bronze spots. Some specimens are intermediate between the two color forms. In both phases the belly is mottled with a white and gray "salt and pepper" pattern.

Adult length: 2.25 to 5 inches (5.7 to 12.7 cm).

SIMILAR SPECIES:

The four-toed salamander (page 50) has a white belly with black spots and only four toes on each hind foot. The red-backed salamander has five toes on each hind foot.

DISTRIBUTION AND STATUS:

Red-backed salamanders are common in suitable habitat throughout

Adult

"Redback" and
"leadback" phases.

R.W. VanDevender

Michigan. Both color phases can be found anywhere in the state but vary in relative abundance.

HABITAT AND HABITS:

Red-backed salamanders live in woodlands, particularly those with decaying logs and thick leaf litter. A moist environment is required because they lack lungs and "breathe" entirely through their moist skins. This salamander can survive where there are no nearby ponds or other water habitats, as it has no aquatic larval stage.

Red-backed salamanders mate mostly in the fall. During courtship the male secretes a substance from a gland on his chin that is rubbed on the female's head and nostrils to stimulate her to breed. Eventually he deposits a spermatophore that the female picks up with her cloaca to fertilize the eggs.

In June the female lays from three to fourteen eggs in a cavity within a log, beneath a rock, or underground. The eggs usually hang from the top of the nest cavity and are attended by the female. She keeps them moist and protects them from mold and predators. Red-backed salamander larvae complete their development within the egg. The baby salamanders usually hatch in August and look like miniatures of the adults, though they may have tiny gill buds that are soon absorbed. The young may remain with the mother for several days or weeks after hatching. Two years are usually required to reach breeding size.

These salamanders eat small invertebrates, including ants, beetles, spiders, earthworms, centipedes, and snails.

Red-backed salamanders often defend their home areas against others of their species. Females guarding eggs will snap and bite at other salamanders that approach the nest area. A red-backed salamander can drop all or part of its tail if attacked by a predator. The wiggling tail may distract the attacker long enough to allow the salamander to escape. It later grows a new tail that is often lighter in color than the original.

Red-backed salamanders must live in moist habitats.

FOUR-TOED SALAMANDER

Hemidactylium scutatum

DESCRIPTION:

This is a tiny, slender, reddish brown salamander with a long tail. The tail narrows distinctly where it joins the body. The belly is white with distinct black spots. Sometimes there is black mottling on the sides and tail. There are four toes on each hind foot.

Adult length: 2 to 4 inches (5 to 10.2 cm).

SIMILAR SPECIES:

The red-backed salamander (page 46) has five toes on the hind foot, and its tail is not constricted where it joins the body.

DISTRIBUTION AND STATUS:

Four-toed salamanders have been found in both peninsulas of Michigan. Though generally uncommon, they can be locally common in places with ideal habitat.

FOUR-TOED SALAMANDER

Adult

R.W. VanDevender

The belly showing its distinct black spots.

R.W. VanDevender

HABITAT AND HABITS:

This species inhabits moist woodlands with boggy ponds or creeks, tamarack and sphagnum bogs, and conifer swamps. They are most common in shady, undisturbed forests with shallow ponds edged with moss and rotting logs. Adult four-toed salamanders are terrestrial and are sometimes found under logs with red-backed salamanders. Unlike the red-backed, however, their larvae are fully aquatic.

Mating in this species takes place on land. Courtship is similar to that of the red-backed salamander (page 46). In spring the female moves to a nesting site at the edge of a pond or stream. Here she lays 15 to 40 or more eggs in a cavity under or within a clump of moss or in rotting wood. The eggs are attended by the female for at least part of the incubation period. During this time she eats spoiled eggs and her skin secretions may help protect the eggs against mold and fungal growth. Communal nests (containing eggs from two or more females) may occur, especially if nest sites are scarce. The nest is situated so that the larvae fall into the water when they hatch. Incubation takes from 38 to 62 days.

The half-inch-long (1.2 cm) larvae eat tiny invertebrates and double in size in about six weeks, when they are ready to metamorphose to the terrestrial form. Young four-toed salamanders reach maturity in their third year when they are about 2 inches (5 cm) long.

Four-toed salamanders feed on small invertebrates, mainly insects and spiders.

These salamanders can voluntarily drop their tails when threatened. The tail breaks off easily at its constricted base and wiggles vigorously, which may attract the attention of the predator while the salamander escapes. It later grows a new tail.

Eggs of the four-toed salamander within a clump of moss (left) and attended by the female (right).

EASTERN AMERICAN TOAD
Bufo americanus americanus

DESCRIPTION:

Toads are short, stocky amphibians with dry, warty skins and relatively short legs. Unlike most frogs, they make short hops rather than long leaps. American toads can be gray, brown, reddish brown, tan, or olive, and usually have dark spots on the back which encircle one or two (rarely more) of the larger warts. There is often dark spotting on the otherwise whitish or yellowish throat and belly.

Adult length: 2 to 4.37 inches (5.1 to 11.1 cm).

SIMILAR SPECIES:

Fowler's toad (page 58) usually has more spots on the back, with each large spot encircling three or more warts, and a plain, unspotted, whitish underside (sometimes with a single dark spot on the chest). The low-pitched, nasal breeding call of the male Fowler's toad is very different from the high-pitched trill of the American.

EASTERN AMERICAN TOAD

Adult

Male toad calling.

Tadpoles

DISTRIBUTION AND STATUS:

The American toad occurs throughout Michigan. They can be common even in suburban areas as long as shallow ponds are available for breeding, but toads quickly disappear if these small wetlands are drained or polluted.

HABITAT AND HABITS:

American toads typically inhabit open woodlands and wood edges but also occur in meadows, marshes, lakeshores, and suburban gardens. They are often seen moving about on rainy or humid nights, but hot, dry periods and the winter months are spent buried in moist soil or plant debris. Toads back into their burrows, using their hind feet as shovels.

From early April to early May, males move to ponds, ditches, sloughs, or floodings and begin calling from the shoreline or shallow water. The call is a long, high-pitched trill which lasts up to 30 seconds and is given with the throat sac fully inflated. The first males to call attract both females and other males to the pond. Males will try to clasp any other toad, but other males give a chirping release call that informs the first one of his mistake.

A female is clasped behind her front legs in an embrace called amplexus. From this position the male can fertilize the eggs as they are laid by the female. The eggs, which number from 2,000 to over 20,000, emerge in long gelatinous strings that are twined around submerged sticks and plants.

The tiny, black tadpoles hatch in three to fourteen days, depending on water temperature. They may form large schools, concentrating in warm, shallow water. Tadpoles feed on algae, other plant material, and carrion (including dead tadpoles), and grow quickly, transforming into little (.25 to .5 inch-long) toadlets in about six to ten weeks. In late June or early July, newly metamorphosed toads may swarm by the hundreds around the edges of the breeding ponds, but few of these bite-sized creatures survive their first weeks out of the water. Those that do survive reach maturity in two to three years.

American toads eat a wide variety of insects, as well as spiders and earthworms, and are useful animals to have in a garden. One researcher found that a modest-sized toad might eat an average of 26 insects a day between May and August, or about 3,200 insects in the season.

Toads have many defenses against predators, beginning with their earth-tone colors and a habit of staying buried much of the time. If attacked, they can produce a noxious secretion from the large warts on their backs. This substance irritates mucous membranes and can be poisonous to small mammals if ingested, but many snakes and predatory birds eat toads. Other toad defenses include inflating themselves with air (making them difficult for smaller predators to swallow) and squirting urine. Toads often urinate when picked up but can be safely handled by humans. (Avoid getting toad skin secretions into your eyes, nose, or mouth.) Toads do not cause warts.

FOWLER'S TOAD
Bufo woodhousii fowleri

DESCRIPTION:

Fowler's toads are brown, gray, olive green, or tan, usually with a number of large, irregular dark spots on the back. Most of the large spots contain three or more warts. The belly is usually whitish, sometimes with a dark spot or a few spots on the chest.

Adult length: 2 to 3.75 inches (5 to 9.5 cm).

SIMILAR SPECIES:

Eastern American toads (page 54) usually have only one or two warts in each dark spot on the back, and they have heavier spotting on the throat and upper belly. The long, trilled breeding call of the American toad is very different from the shorter, more nasal call of the Fowler's.

DISTRIBUTION AND STATUS:

Fowler's toad is restricted to the western and southern counties of the Lower Peninsula. Within this range it is generally less common than the American toad

58

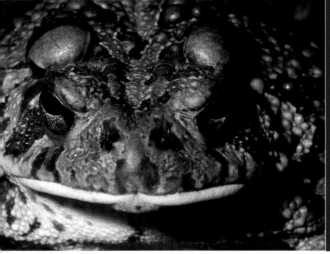

Light-colored adult (above).

Front view (left).

but can be locally common, particularly in counties bordering Lake Michigan. This species will hybridize with the American toad, but the extent to which this occurs in Michigan is unknown.

HABITAT AND HABITS:

Fowler's toads prefer open woods and fields, particularly those with sandy soils. These toads are a characteristic species of Lake Michigan dune woodlands. Like the American toad, Fowler's toad burrows into the ground during hot, dry periods and in winter, but they are more likely to be active in the daytime.

Breeding habits of Fowler's toads are similar to those of American toads (page 54), except that they prefer warmer temperatures and breed later in spring, usually mid-May to mid-June. The voice of the male Fowler's toad is a low-pitched, nasal "waaaa" which can carry for a considerable distance. Each call lasts from one to four seconds. The eggs are laid in long gelatinous strings during amplexus, and hatch in two to seven days. Metamorphosis can occur as soon as a month after hatching. The tad-poles and newly transformed toadlets of this species are almost identical in appearance to those of the American toad.

Fowler's toads eat insects, spiders, and other small invertebrates. Like the American toad, this species has toxic skin secretions for defense (see page 57). Some specimens, if roughly handled, will lie motionless on their backs and "play dead."

Fowler's toad

BLANCHARD'S CRICKET FROG

Acris crepitans blanchardi

DESCRIPTION:

This is a tiny frog with moist, warty skin and a pointed snout. They have relatively long hind legs, with a dark stripe on the inner thigh. Cricket frogs can be brown, tan, or olive green on the upper surfaces. Most have a dark, triangle-shaped mark (pointed backward) between the eyes. Some may have a green, brown, or reddish stripe down the back.

Adult length: .75 to 1.5 inches (2 to 3.8 cm).

SIMILAR SPECIES:

The western chorus frog (page 66) has a whitish stripe along the upper lip and brownish stripes on the sides and back. The spring peeper is not warty and usually has an X-shaped mark on the back.

DISTRIBUTION AND STATUS:

Blanchard's cricket frog formerly occurred over much of the southern half of Michigan's Lower Peninsula. There

Adult

In habitat

are a number of unconfirmed records for the northern Lower Peninsula. This species has declined in numbers over most of its range in the state and has disappeared from many places where it once lived. Blanchard's cricket frogs are listed as a "special concern" species by the Michigan Department of Natural Resources and are protected by state wildlife regulations.

HABITAT AND HABITS:

Blanchard's cricket frogs inhabit the edges of permanent ponds, lakes, floodings, and streams. Open or partly vegetated mud flats adjacent to the water seem to be a preferred habitat. You may see these frogs jumping erratically ahead as you walk along the shoreline. These random zigzag leaps may help them escape predators. If frightened into the water, they may jump or swim immediately back to shore or dive to the bottom and hide in the mud.

In Michigan, cricket frogs breed from late May through mid-July. The male's call sounds like pebbles being clicked together with increasing tempo. Amplexus and egg laying occur in warm, shallow water near the calling sites. From 200 to 400 eggs are attached to submerged plants or twigs, either singly or in small clusters. The tadpoles are distinctive, being olive or brown, speckled with black, and with a long, low tail fin with a black tip. Metamorphosis occurs five to ten weeks after hatching, usually in July or August. The newly transformed froglets are tiny—often under a half-inch (1.3 cm) long—but can reach breeding size the following spring.

Blanchard's cricket frogs eat small invertebrates, mostly insects, and feed both day and night. It has been estimated that one cricket frog can eat around 4,800 insects annually.

Male cricket frog calling.

WESTERN CHORUS FROG

Pseudacris triseriata triseriata

DESCRIPTION:

The western chorus frog is a very small, striped frog with a light line along its upper lip. A dark stripe runs from the snout through the eye and along the side to the groin. Usually there are three other dark brown or gray stripes running down the back, but these may be broken into rows of spots. The basic color can be brown, tan, gray, olive, or (rarely) rusty orange. They have a whitish belly. The ends of the toes are slightly expanded into small discs. NOTE: The boreal chorus frog (*Pseudacris triseriata maculata*) is a western subspecies found in Michigan only on Isle Royale. It is very similar to the western but has relatively shorter hind legs.

Adult length: .75 to 1.5 inches (1.9 to 3.8 cm).

SIMILAR SPECIES:

The spring peeper (page 70) lacks the light line on the lip and usually has an X-shaped marking on the back. The wood

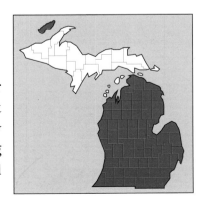

WESTERN CHORUS FROG

Adult

The adult is approximately .75 to 1.5 inches long.

frog (page 98) is much larger and has dorsolateral folds (a ridge of skin down each side of the back).

DISTRIBUTION AND STATUS:

The western chorus frog occurs throughout Michigan's Lower Peninsula. These frogs can be common even in farming and suburban areas, but their numbers are declining in some areas. Chorus frogs seem to be absent from the Upper Peninsula mainland. As previously noted, the boreal chorus frog has been recorded on Isle Royale in western Lake Superior.

HABITAT AND HABITS:

Chorus frogs live in a variety of habitats, including marshes, meadows, fallow farm fields, and damp woodlands. They are rarely seen after the breeding season but are occasionally found under logs or boards in moist places.

This is usually the first frog species to call in spring, in some years as early as mid-March. They appear to overwinter near their breeding sites, which include vernal ponds, flooded fields, ditches, marsh edges, and wooded swamps. The voice of the male is a short, rising, squeaky trill that may be imitated by strumming the small teeth of a stiff pocket comb from middle to end with a thumbnail. Amplexus and egg laying occur mostly in April, but reproduction can extend into late May. Females produce from 500 to 1,500 eggs laid in small gelatinous masses of 20 to 100 or more eggs attached to underwater grasses and twigs. The tadpoles hatch in three to fourteen days and metamorphose into tiny froglets six to eight weeks later.

Chorus frogs eat a variety of small insects, spiders, and other invertebrates. The tadpoles feed mostly on algae.

Chorus frogs live in marshes, meadows, fallow farm fields, and damp woodlands.

NORTHERN SPRING PEEPER

Pseudacris crucifer crucifer

DESCRIPTION:

Spring peepers are very small, brown or tan treefrogs with small adhesive pads on the tips of their toes. Most peepers have an X-shaped mark on the back, but the "X" may be incomplete or broken. There is usually a dark line between the eyes, and the belly is whitish or cream colored.

Adult length: .75 to 1.38 inches (1.9 to 3.5 cm).

SIMILAR SPECIES:

Western chorus frogs (page 66) have a light line on the lip and lack an X-shaped mark on the back.

DISTRIBUTION AND STATUS:

The spring peeper is common in suitable habitat throughout both Michigan peninsulas.

HABITAT AND HABITS:

These frogs inhabit swamps, woodlands, and overgrown meadows. They

Adult

Calling male

Pair in amplexus.

are rarely seen after the spring breeding season, which lasts from late March through May. Breeding sites include woodland ponds, marshes, floodings, and other shallow bodies of water. Male peepers emit a high-pitched "peep!" call to attract females, and a large chorus of peepers can seem almost deafening to people nearby. Males also give a lower-pitched trilled call that may be a warning to other males that intrude into their calling territories. Females appear to discriminate between males based on the strength of the calls, perhaps showing a preference for larger (louder) males.

During amplexus, a female peeper attaches up to 1,000 eggs to underwater leaves or stems, either singly or in small rows or clusters. The eggs hatch in three to fifteen days, and the brownish tadpoles transform into tiny froglets two to three months later.

Spring peepers are sometimes heard calling in late summer or fall, often while they are some distance from the breeding ponds. Females are not ready to breed at this time, and the reasons for late season calling are unknown.

Peepers eat small invertebrates, such as insects, spiders, and mites, and will climb into bushes and other vegetation to pursue prey. They pass the winter buried under leaf litter, rotting logs, or other forest debris. Peepers are one of the frog species known to survive partial freezing of body fluids.

Spring peepers often breed in constructed ponds.

GRAY TREEFROG
Hyla versicolor and *Hyla chrysoscelis*

IDENTIFICATION:

Gray treefrogs have moist, warty skin and large adhesive toe pads. They can be gray, green, or brown and can change between various shades of these colors. Most have irregular dark blotches on the back and legs and a white spot beneath each eye. The belly is white, and the underside of the hind legs and groin is bright golden yellow.

Adult length: 1.25 to 2.4 inches (3.2 to 6 cm).

SIMILAR SPECIES:

Two nearly identical species of gray treefrogs occur in Michigan. There is no reliable way to separate them based on size, coloration, or habits, but it is often possible to identify them while they are calling in spring. At the same body temperature, male eastern gray treefrogs (*Hyla versicolor*) have a slow, musical trill, while Cope's gray treefrogs (*Hyla chrysoscelis*) have a shorter, lower-pitched nasal trill (see page 111). Distinguishing the two species is easiest when

GRAY TREEFROG

Adult

Green and gray *Hyla versicolor*

Tadpole

R. W. VanDevender

75

they are calling together, allowing direct comparison. Positive identification requires blood sampling and laboratory analysis. *Hyla versicolor*, a genetic tetraploid, has twice the number of chromosomes as the diploid species *Hyla chrysoscelis*.

DISTRIBUTION AND STATUS:

Gray treefrogs are locally common throughout both peninsulas. Although the eastern gray treefrog is more widely distributed in Michigan than the Cope's, the relative distribution of these two species is poorly known.

HABITAT AND HABITS:

Damp woods and wooded swamps are favored by these treefrogs, but they adapt quite well to farmlands and suburban areas. Their large, sticky toe pads make them excellent climbers, and they can climb high in trees and shrubs. Gray treefrogs are often seen at night clinging to windows or sitting under outdoor lights where they eat insects attracted to the light.

Gray treefrogs breed from late April through June, but most egg laying occurs from mid-May to early June. Breeding sites include woodland ponds, swamps, marshes, and shallow lake margins. Males give their trills while perched in clumps of vegetation over or near water, usually after dark, or on humid, overcast days. Air temperatures of 60°F (15.5°C) or higher are normally needed to stimulate calling.

The female gray treefrog chooses her mate by approaching a singing male, which then clasps her behind the front legs. As the joined pair floats on the water's surface, the female lays up to 2,000 eggs divided into loose gelatinous clusters containing up to 40 eggs. Hatching occurs in three to six days. Gray treefrog tadpoles have greenish bodies and high, reddish tail fins with black spots along the edge. They are often seen feeding at the water's surface, hanging tail downward. The tadpoles metamorphose into tiny (half-inch-long) treefroglets in six to eight weeks. Newly transformed gray treefrogs are usually green and tend to stay near their ponds during the first summer.

Gray treefrogs may call long after the breeding season, often from high in the trees during humid or rainy weather. These frogs pass the winter months by digging into leaf litter or rotted wood, or hiding in tree crevices or hollows. They are able to survive subfreezing temperatures by producing a natural body antifreeze.

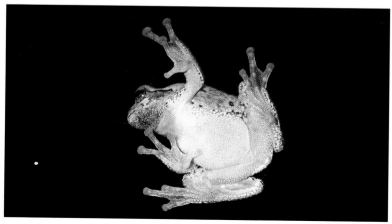

Gray treefrogs are often seen clinging to windows at night.

GREEN FROG

Rana clamitans melanota

DESCRIPTION:

Green frogs may be green, yellowish green, olive, or brown, and often have some dark spots on the back and sides and dark bands across the legs. Upper Peninsula green frogs tend to be more heavily spotted than those from farther south. A ridge of skin (the dorsolateral fold) starts at the top of each eardrum and extends at least partway down the back. The belly is white, often with grayish mottling. In adult males the eardrum is larger than the eye and the throat is bright yellow. The female's eardrum is about the size of the eye and the throat is white or pale yellow.

Adult length: 2.3 to 4.25 inches (5.8 to 10.8 cm).

SIMILAR SPECIES:

The bullfrog (page 82) lacks dorsolateral folds on its back. The mink frog (U.P. only, page 94) often lacks dorsolateral folds and usually has dark spots or lengthwise streaks on the legs, not crossbars as in green frogs. Mink frogs produce a musky odor when handled.

GREEN FROG

Adult female

Adult male

Egg mass

Tadpole

DISTRIBUTION AND STATUS:

Green frogs are the most conspicuous frogs in Michigan and are common throughout the state. This species is occasionally used as human food, but few green frogs grow large enough to warrant harvesting them. Michigan law regulates the taking of frogs through bag limits and a closed season. Check with the Department of Natural Resources for current rules.

HABITAT AND HABITS:

Green frogs are found in and around most inland waters, including ponds, lakes, marshes, wooded swamps, and the banks of streams and rivers. Adults tend to stay near the water, but juveniles disperse widely through woods and meadows during rainy weather. A startled green frog often gives a loud squawk as it leaps into the water.

Breeding begins in mid-May and extends well into the summer. Males defend prime breeding sites in shallow, weedy, permanent waters and have a variety of calls related to maintaining territories and attracting mates. Their single-note advertisement call ("clung!") sounds like a plucked banjo string. If other males are detected nearby, this "banjo" call may be given several times in a row with great intensity. If an intruder enters his territory, the male may emit a series of growl-like warning notes followed by a sharp single "clung!" A resident male will attack a determined invader, and growl-like sounds may be given as the frogs wrestle for possession of the territory.

A female green frog probably chooses her mate because his territory is desirable as an egg-laying site. During amplexus, up to 5,000 eggs are laid in a large, loose mass that floats on the surface or hangs in aquatic vegetation. The eggs hatch in about three to six days. The olive-green, black-speckled tadpoles mainly eat algae and other plant life but do some scavenging as well. When their front legs appear, the tadpoles stop feeding until their tails are absorbed. Tadpoles that hatch early in the season may metamorphose in late summer, but many overwinter as tadpoles and become froglets the following spring or summer. Four or five years are required to reach full adult size.

Green frogs mostly eat insects and other invertebrates, but large adults will eat smaller frogs, including young green frogs. These frogs overwinter underwater, either resting on the bottom or concealed in mud or under submerged objects.

On occasion, green frogs lack yellow pigment in their skins and are blue in color.

BULLFROG
Rana catesbeiana

DESCRIPTION:

Michigan's largest frog can be green, yellowish green, olive, or brown, sometimes with scattered dark brown spots on the back. The skin may be slightly bumpy, but there are no dorsolateral folds. There are often dark bars on the upper surfaces of the legs. The belly is white, mottled with gray. In adult male bullfrogs the eardrum is much larger than the eye and the throat is yellow. Females have smaller eardrums (about the size of the eye) and white throats.

Adult length: 3.5 to 8 inches (9 to 20.3 cm).

SIMILAR SPECIES:

The green frog (page 78) has dorsolateral folds (ridges) along both sides of the back.

DISTRIBUTION AND STATUS:

Bullfrogs are found throughout Michigan, though their numbers have reportedly declined in parts of the state in

BULLFROG

Adult male

Adult female

Tadpole

R.W. VanDevender

R.W. VanDevender

recent years. Overharvesting has undoubtedly contributed to this decline, but environmental factors may also be involved. Michigan law regulates the harvest of frogs with a closed season and bag limits. Check with the Department of Natural Resources for current rules before capturing frogs.

HABITAT AND HABITS:

Bullfrogs inhabit permanent ponds, lakes, marshes, sloughs, and impoundments. They are most common in warm waters with abundant plant growth.

Bullfrogs are normally the last species of frog to become active in spring. Breeding activity usually begins in June and may continue into early July. Male bullfrogs give a very low-pitched, resonating call that sounds like "brrr-rr-rr-rum." Calling males often sit upright in the water with their yellow throats inflated—probably as a warning to rivals or to attract females. The males are territorial and aggressively defend their calling sites against other males. If the short one- or two-note warning call is not enough to discourage a challenger, a resident male may attack his rival. A bullfrog fight resembles a wrestling match, with the combatants attempting to hold each other underwater or push each other out of the area.

The female bullfrog chooses her mate by swimming to the calling male, but once in amplexus the paired frogs may move to another location for egg laying. Each female lays from 5,000 to over 20,000 eggs in a thin floating mass that may cover an area up to five square feet. The eggs hatch in three to six days. The tadpoles are greenish with black spots and a white belly and eat mostly algae. They grow rapidly, sometimes reaching a length of up to 6 inches (15.2 cm). Most overwinter as tadpoles and do not metamorphose until their second summer, and some require a third year before transformation.

Bullfrogs eat nearly any animal that they can swallow, including insects, crayfish, smaller frogs, fish, small snakes and turtles, mice, and birds. In turn, these frogs and their tadpoles are eaten by many predators. Because of their large size, bullfrogs are often harvested by humans for frog legs. The long time required for bullfrogs to mature, coupled with high natural mortality, makes this species vulnerable to overexploitation.

A bullfrog that is frightened will often give a single "yelp" as it leaps into the water. If grabbed by a predator (or a human), these frogs can give a loud, wailing scream. This may startle an attacker long enough to allow the frog to escape.

W. Leonard

Bullfrog tadpole

NORTHERN LEOPARD FROG

Rana pipiens

DESCRIPTION:

This is a medium-sized, brown or green frog with rounded dark spots on the back and sides. The spots are usually outlined with lighter color. There are conspicuous dorsolateral folds and a light line on each upper jaw, from the nose to the shoulder. The belly is white or cream colored, sometimes with a faint yellowish tint in the groin area.

Adult length: 2 to 4.4 inches (5 to 11.1 cm).

SIMILAR SPECIES:

The pickerel frog (page 90) has squarish instead of rounded spots and bright yellowish orange color on the groin and undersides of the hind legs.

DISTRIBUTION AND STATUS:

Northern leopard frogs are found throughout Michigan. At one time this was the most abundant frog in the state, but populations declined drastically during the 1970s for unknown reasons.

NORTHERN LEOPARD FROG

Adult

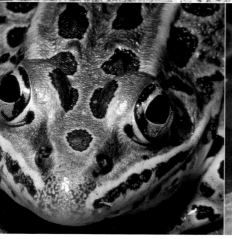

W. Blinn

Paired vocal sacs.

Leopard frogs are locally common in some parts of the state but remain scarce in many areas where they were once abundant.

HABITAT AND HABITS:

Leopard frogs inhabit marshes, meadows, and the grassy edges of ponds, lakes, and streams. In summer they may wander well away from water.

Breeding usually occurs in April in ponds, weedy lakes, and deeper marsh pools. The male's advertisement call sounds like a low snore punctuated by several hoarse clucks and croaks. They usually call while floating on the surface in concealing vegetation, or sometimes while submerged. Males have two vocal sacs, one on each side behind the mouth, which inflate during calling.

During amplexus the female deposits one or more rounded gelatinous masses of eggs which are attached to sticks or vegetation below the water's surface. Each egg cluster contains from 3,500 to 6,000 eggs which are fertilized by the male as they are laid. Hatching occurs in one to three weeks, depending on water temperature. The tadpoles are green or olive green above and whitish on the belly. They feed mostly on algae and can grow to a length of about 3 inches (7.6 cm). By July or August most of the tadpoles have transformed into tiny inch-long froglets, although a few may overwinter as tadpoles and transform the following spring. Leopard frogs reach breeding size in one or two years after metamorphosis.

Very young leopard frogs tend to stay close to the water during their first summer, but adults disperse widely into fields and gardens. Leopard frogs feed mainly on insects and are undoubtedly of great value to farmers and gardeners. They return to water in fall and spend the winter buried in mud or lying on the bottom of ponds, lakes, and streams.

Leopard frogs and their tadpoles are eaten by a great number of predators, including fish, snakes, snapping turtles, larger frogs, hawks, herons, and mammals such as raccoons, minks, and otters. An adult frog will make long, erratic leaps to escape an enemy and, if grabbed, can emit a loud scream that might startle its attacker.

Brown adult

PICKEREL FROG

Rana palustris

DESCRIPTION:

Pickerel frogs are brown or green with two irregular rows of squarish dark spots down the back and additional spots on the sides and legs. They have distinct, light-colored dorsolateral folds and a light line along the upper jaw. The belly is whitish, and the groin and undersides of the hind legs are bright yellow or orange.

Adult length: 1.75 to 3.43 inches (4.4 to 8.7 cm).

SIMILAR SPECIES:

The northern leopard frog (page 86) has rounded spots and lacks bright yellow or orange color under the hind legs.

DISTRIBUTION AND STATUS:

The pickerel frog is found throughout Michigan. They are generally uncommon but can be locally common in ideal habitat. These frogs are sensitive to changes in water quality and disappear from polluted waters.

PICKEREL FROG

Adult (above)

Underside showing whitish belly and bright yellow orange under the hind legs (left).

HABITAT AND HABITS:

Pickerel frogs inhabit grassy or marshy edges of bogs, lakes, springs, and streams. They prefer cooler waters than do northern leopard frogs and are less likely to move long distances from water.

Pickerel frogs breed in April and early May. The male's advertisement call sounds like a low-pitched snore, similar to the leopard frog's call (page 86) but shorter and softer, with less carrying power. They can call either while floating on the surface or submerged. The female lays her eggs in a rounded gelatinous cluster attached to submerged sticks or plant stems. The tadpoles hatch in 10 to 14 days and metamorphose about two to three months later. The newly transformed froglets are about 1 inch (2.5 cm) long.

Pickerel frogs eat a variety of insects, spiders, snails, worms, and other invertebrates. This species produces a noxious skin secretion that is poisonous or at least distasteful to many predators, such as snakes and birds. However, bullfrogs and green frogs appear to eat pickerel frogs without effect. Handling pickerel frogs does not harm humans, but avoid getting the skin secretions into your eyes, mouth, or mucous membranes.

Pickerel frogs inhabit the edges of bogs, lakes, springs, and streams.

MINK FROG

Rana septentrionalis

DESCRIPTION:

Mink frogs are greenish, olive, or brown, with either scattered, dark, rounded spots or a heavier pattern of irregular blotches. The upper surfaces of the legs have spots or lengthwise stripes, and the upper "lips" are plain green. The dorsolateral folds may be nearly complete, broken, or lacking completely. Male mink frogs have eardrums which are larger than the eye, but the eardrums of females are the same size or smaller than the eye. The belly is whitish, sometimes grading to yellowish on the sides and chin. When handled, these frogs give off a musky odor that resembles the smell of a mink, though some describe it as smelling like rotten onions.

Adult length: 2 to 3 inches (5 to 7.6 cm).

SIMILAR SPECIES:

Green frogs (page 78) usually have complete dorsolateral folds and crossbands (not spots or stripes) on the hind legs and do not have a musky odor when handled. Green frogs in the Upper Pen-

MINK FROG

Adult

Mink frog (left) with green frog (right).

Adult

insula often have a dark mottled pattern resembling that of a mink frog and occasionally may have dorso-lateral folds that are incomplete or nearly lacking. Hybridization between green and mink frogs may occur, but research is needed to confirm this.

DISTRIBUTION AND STATUS:

In Michigan the mink frog is found only in the Upper Peninsula, where they are locally common.

HABITAT AND HABITS:

Mink frogs occur in ponds, bogs, and lakes, and along slow-moving streams or backwaters. They prefer waters with abundant emergent vegetation such as lily pads and pickerel weed, or cool, boggy places near lake inlets and outlets. They usually stay in or near water and are wary and difficult to approach.

The breeding season for mink frogs extends from early June through July. The male's mating call is a low-pitched "tok, tok, tok, tok" which can sound like distant hammering. During amplexus, a female lays from 1,000 to 4,000 eggs in a rounded gelatinous mass attached to vegetation beneath the surface. The greenish, black-spotted tadpoles spend one or two years as larvae before they transform into froglets about 1.2 to 1.6 inches (3 to 4 cm) long. Permanent water is required for mink frog reproduction.

Mink frogs eat a variety of insects and other invertebrates, many of which are aquatic species. In turn, these frogs and their tadpoles provide food for fish, raccoons, herons, and other predators. Like related species, mink frogs may give a loud shriek when startled or grabbed. A frightened mink frog may flee over deep water by leaping on lily pads before diving beneath the surface. The musky-smelling skin secretion of mink frogs is presumably distasteful to some predators.

Mink frogs occur in ponds, bogs, and lakes, and along slow-moving streams or backwaters.

WOOD FROG

Rana sylvatica

DESCRIPTION:

This is a brown, reddish brown, or tan frog with a dark "mask" behind each eye. There is a white line along the upper lip, and the conspicuous dorsolateral folds may be spotted with black. Some wood frogs, especially those from northern areas, have a light stripe down the middle of the back. The belly is white, sometimes with grayish mottling, and the hind legs may have dark crossbands. Male wood frogs are often very dark brown to almost black while in breeding ponds in spring and tend to be darker and smaller than females thoughout the year. In males, the webbing between the hind toes is straight edged or curved outward, while in females the webbing usually curves inward.

Adult length: 1.35 to 3.25 inches (3.4 to 8.3 cm).

SIMILAR SPECIES:

The western chorus frog (page 66) is much smaller, has brownish stripes on the back, and slightly expanded toe tips, and lacks dorsolateral folds.

98

WOOD FROG

Adult

R. W. VanDevender

Tadpole

Egg mass

R. W. VanDevender

DISTRIBUTION AND STATUS:

Wood frogs are common throughout Michigan in suitable habitat.

HABITAT AND HABITS:

This frog is well named as it is found in a variety of wooded habitats, from the coniferous and mixed hardwood forests of northern Michigan to farm woodlots and floodplain swamp woods in the south. They soon disappear when moist, shady environments are eliminated.

Wood frogs breed in early spring, moving to temporary woodland ponds, bogs, and floodings in late March and early April, sometimes while patches of snow are still on the ground. Males float on the surface while giving their cluck-like calls. From a distance, a group of calling wood frogs can sound like quacking ducks. The females move to the breeding sites quickly, and the majority of egg laying occurs within a short time, usually a week to ten days unless cold weather forces a delay.

Although calling males distribute themselves throughout the breeding pond, paired frogs in amplexus often move to a deeper part of the pond before the eggs are laid. This is often a communal site where a large number of egg masses are deposited in a small area by most wood frogs in the pond. Several reasons for this communal nesting have been suggested. One idea is that the glut of potential food may assure that egg predators will be unable to destroy all of the eggs before hatching. It is also possible that the large number of dark-colored eggs absorb heat faster and hold heat longer than single egg masses.

Each female lays from 800 to 3,000 eggs in one or more rounded masses attached to underwater vegetation or debris. The eggs hatch in one to three weeks, depending on water temperature. Tadpoles are brown or olive brown, often with black and gold flecks. Their bellies may appear pinkish, with the digestive organs showing through the skin. The tadpoles transform into froglets in 45 to 80 days. In drought years, many wood frog tadpoles die as ponds dry up before metamorphosis can occur.

Wood frogs leave the water after breeding and spend the summer on the forest floor, where they eat insects, spiders, and other small invertebrates. Their brownish colors blend in well with leaf litter. When disturbed, they usually make long, erratic leaps and then freeze, often seeming to suddenly disappear.

Wood frogs from the Upper Peninsula often have a dorsal stripe.

NOTES ON BIOLOGY

RELATIONSHIPS OF FROGS, TOADS, AND SALAMANDERS

Frogs, toads, and salamanders are amphibians, members of the class Amphibia. The word "amphibian" comes from the Greek language and means "double life," referring to the fact that most amphibians begin life as aquatic gilled larvae and eventually transform into animals capable of living on land. Amphibians evolved from fishes over 360 million years ago, and a branch of the amphibia gave rise to the reptiles about 315 million years ago.

No longer continuously supported by water like their fish ancestors, early amphibians evolved several skeletal changes to compensate for the increased pull of gravity. These included strong limbs and limb girdles, expanded vertebrae (backbones), and a rib cage to protect internal organs.

Living amphibians are placed in three main groups (orders). The frogs and toads (order Anura) and salamanders (order Caudata) are found worldwide in both temperate and tropical regions. The legless, wormlike caecilians (order Gymnophiona) are confined to tropical regions.

There are nearly 3,500 species of frogs and toads, collectively called anurans by biologists. How can we tell a frog from a toad? Generally, warty, short-legged, hopping anurans are called toads, and smooth-skinned, jumping anurans are called frogs. However, there are many species worldwide that fall somewhere between these definitions. In Michigan there are two species of true toads and eleven species of anurans commonly called frogs.

Salamanders are less specialized than frogs and toads and more closely resemble the ancient amphibians that first conquered the land. Salamanders generally prefer cool, moist habitats and thus are most abundant in the temperate regions of the world, though a few of the approximately 360 species are found in the tropics.

Frogs, toads, and salamanders have several characteristics that suggest they are closely related. For example, their teeth are unlike those of other vertebrate animals. These teeth

R. W. VanDevender

Most amphibians, like this spotted salamander, live in moist habitats.

consist of two parts—a base (pedicel) and a pointed crown that fits on top of the base but is not completely fused to it. Other shared characteristics include special ear and eye structures, fat bodies connected to the reproductive organs, special features of the skin and lungs, and genetic similarities. However, some paleontologists think that frogs and salamanders evolved from separate types of primitive amphibians.

FOSSIL HISTORY OF FROGS AND TOADS

Frogs and toads have a poor fossil record, probably because their bones are small and fragile. The fossil of the earliest known frog-like animal, *Triadobatrachus*, was found on the island of Madagascar in sediments of the early Triassic Period, dating from about 230 million years ago. The head of this animal was very frog-like, but the body was longer and the hip bones were smaller than those found in modern frogs. It may not have been able to jump.

All living families of frogs and toads appeared early in the Age of Mammals (Tertiary Period of the Cenozoic Era), and species very similar to those that occur in Michigan today were present by the early Miocene Epoch, about

30 million years ago. After these modern kinds of frogs and toads evolved, they appear to have changed very little, at least in temperate parts of the world.

BASIC BODY PLAN OF FROGS AND TOADS

Adult frogs and toads have a specialized body plan that is quite different from that of the earliest amphibians. The head is large and wide, and the eye sockets and eyes are often very large. The body is short and tailless, and they have many cartilaginous (non-bony and flexible) parts in their skeletons. The hind limbs and

Northern leopard frog.

limb supports (pelvic girdle) are very long, associated with the ability to jump or hop.

Most frogs and toads (including all Michigan ones) actually exist as two different creatures—a larva (tadpole) and an adult. The early stages of frog and toad larvae are fishlike, with no limbs, and have compressed tails used for swimming. They breathe with gills, although the gills are internal. Tadpoles lack true teeth, but they do have toothlike structures arranged in rows around the mouth.

During the gradual metamorphosis into adult form, dramatic changes take place. Internally, the digestive system changes from a vegetarian type to a carnivorous type and lungs develop to replace the gills. Externally, the hind legs appear first, followed later by the front legs, and the tail is absorbed. The head widens as the eyes and mouth get bigger and teeth appear (except in true toads, which are toothless). In tropic, subtropic, and desert areas there are many variations on this pattern of development. For example, a few frog species have no tadpole stage but lay eggs that hatch into tiny froglets resembling miniature adults.

BODY FUNCTIONS OF FROGS AND TOADS

Frogs and toads have lungs, but they also "breathe" through their thin skins, which are full of tiny blood vessels to absorb oxygen. To accomplish this type of breathing, the skin is kept moist by thousands of tiny mucous glands, and most species must live in moist habitats. Toads have a thicker, wartier skin than frogs and lose water more slowly.

Frogs and toads absorb water through their skins and normally do not need to drink water. They cannot live in marine (saltwater) habitats because the salt would quickly dehydrate and kill them. Many desert and tropical species have adapted to resist dehydration. During dry conditions some species burrow into the mud and form a protective cocoon around themselves with thick mucous or several layers of shed skin. Many anurans burrow deep into the ground during extended dry periods, sometimes for a year or more.

The skins of frogs and toads possess tiny poison glands that, in some species, produce substances that can harm or kill predators that try to eat them. In some parts of the world there are species that are potentially deadly. For

Poison dart frog.

instance, the small poison dart frogs of tropical forests in Central and South America have skin secretions so toxic that some native people use them on blow gun darts and arrow tips to ensure a quick kill of hunted game animals. The giant toad, *Bufo marinus*, a neotropical species introduced in southern Florida, produces a poison in its parotoid glands that could kill a human if it were swallowed.

In Michigan, few species produce secretions that harm humans or predators. One species, the pickerel frog, is distasteful to many predators, including snakes. A small mammal attempting to eat a native toad might become sick or die from the parotoid secretions. Although picking up a toad or pickerel frog will not harm a person, it is a good idea to keep hands away from the mouth and eyes after handling these amphibians.

Frogs and toads are ectothermic (cold-blooded) and maintain proper body temperatures by moving in and out of sun or shade, by burrowing, or by staying in water (which heats and cools more slowly than air). Overheating is quickly fatal. Frogs and toads avoid freezing in winter by digging deep into the soil or staying underwater. Some Michigan species, including the gray treefrog and the wood frog, can survive temperatures below freezing for short periods by producing a substance that acts like an antifreeze in their bloodstreams.

FOOD AND FEEDING OF FROGS AND TOADS

Michigan frog and toad tadpoles are mainly vegetarians that browse algae and other plant material, but they may also scavenge dead animals, including deceased siblings. Some tadpoles are filter-feeders that sift algae and other particles of food out of the water with their gill structures. In a few mostly tropical or desert species, the larvae are fierce carnivores with strong, beak-like jaws that prey on other tadpoles.

All adult frogs and toads are carnivorous. Small and moderate-sized species feed mainly on insects and other invertebrates. Larger frogs

Bullfrogs will even eat birds if they can catch them.

(green frogs and bullfrogs in Michigan) eat almost any creature they can swallow, including other frogs, small turtles and snakes, rodents, and even birds. Most species sit and wait for food to come by, and the prey animal usually must be moving before it is attacked. Sight is the most important sense that frogs and toads use to find food, but some species search for prey by sound. For example, green frogs can find and eat other species (like the gray treefrog) by locating the singing males.

All Michigan frogs and toads flip out their tongues to capture prey and may use the front feet to stuff large prey into their mouths. In some species the backs of the eyeballs are used to push prey down into the throat, which explains why frogs and toads usually close their eyes while swallowing.

REPRODUCTION OF FROGS AND TOADS

There are many reproductive patterns in frogs worldwide (see the general references listed on page 142), but Michigan frogs and toads follow the basic pattern seen in most temperate climate species. From late winter to early summer (depending on species), the males move to breeding sites in or near shallow, still bodies of water and begin calling. Each species has its own characteristic call, known as an advertisement call, which attracts females of the proper species. These calls may also announce the position of the male frog to other males and warn potential rivals to keep their distance.

R. W. VanDevender

Cope's gray treefrog calling.

When approached by a rival male, a calling frog may change its call to show that it is prepared to defend its territory. Male bullfrogs and green frogs sometimes engage in "wrestling matches," with the victor winning the right to remain in a prime calling spot.

Frogs and toads produce their calls by forcing air from the lungs over the vocal cords. During calling, one or two vocal sacs inflate, which help regulate the characteristics of the call. Some Michigan frogs, such as gray treefrogs, peepers, and toads, have a single vocal sac which bulges in front of the throat. Others, including leopard and wood frogs, have paired sacs that inflate at each side of the throat.

When a male frog or toad succeeds in attracting a female, he grasps her tightly behind the front legs with his front feet in an embrace called amplexus. Sometimes a male will accidentally grasp another male (or a female that has already laid her eggs). In such a case, the mistakenly grasped frog gives a special release call and often vibrates its body to discourage the errant individual. This release call is different from the scream-like distress call given by some frogs when seized by a predator.

During amplexus, the female frog releases her eggs into the water as the male releases sperm to fertilize them. All Michigan frogs and toads fertilize eggs externally. The eggs are small and covered with protective gelatinous (jelly-like) layers which swell in water. Toads lay their eggs in long strings, and frogs may lay eggs singly, in rounded submerged masses, or in spreading surface masses.

The time needed for the eggs to hatch varies, depending on species and water temperature, and ranges from a few days to a week or more. The tadpoles quickly begin feeding and growing. In some species, such as the toads,

Toad eggs (left) and frog eggs (right).

tadpoles may remain in loose groups or schools, while in others the tadpoles are solitary. Most Michigan frogs and toads metamorphose during their first summer, but green frogs may overwinter as tadpoles. Bullfrog tadpoles sometimes require a third summer before changing to adult form.

FOSSIL HISTORY OF SALAMANDERS

The fossil record for salamanders is poorer than that of frogs and toads. The earliest known salamander lived in the late Jurassic Period, about 150 million years ago, but it is likely that salamanders as a group appeared much earlier.

R. W. VanDevender

Bullfrog tadpole

Fossils similar to the living sirens are known from the late Cretaceous Period, during the latter days of the dinosaurs. Newts and mole salamanders were present in the Paleocene Epoch, very early in the Cenozoic Era (Age of Mammals). The lungless salamander group, to which our common Michigan red-backed salamander belongs, appeared about 20 million years ago during the early Miocene Epoch.

BASIC BODY PLAN OF SALAMANDERS

Most adult salamanders have a generalized body plan that more closely resembles ancient amphibian types than does the form of frogs and toads. The head is relatively small, and the eyes are either small or slightly enlarged, though never as large as in most frogs. The legs are short, and the body and tail are elongated.

The differences between larval and adult forms in salamanders are not as distinct as in Michigan frogs and toads. In some species, such as the permanently aquatic mudpuppies and sirens, the adults retain the larval characteristics of external gills and poorly developed eyes. Red-backed salamanders complete the larval stage within the egg and hatch out as miniature versions of the adults. Other Michigan salamanders have larvae with external gills, but these are more like the adult form than are the larvae (tadpoles) of frogs and toads.

BODY FUNCTIONS OF SALAMANDERS

Although most Michigan salamanders have lungs (the red-backed salamander is lungless), these animals breathe through their skins to a great extent, and their thin skins are full of tiny blood vessels. Because salamanders absorb water through the skin, they must live either in water or in moist habitats. Newts have slightly thicker and rougher skins than other Michigan salamanders and lose water more slowly. As a group, salamanders have not adapted to hot or dry conditions as well as certain frogs and toads, and the majority of species live in the moist, temperate parts of the world.

Like frogs, salamanders have many tiny poison glands in their skins which offer protection from predators in some species. These glands are often concentrated on the tail or in large lumps on the head or neck area similar to the

Tail lashing can be used for defense as shown by this blue spotted salamander.

parotoid glands of toads. When attacked, many salamanders will present a predator (such as a snake, shrew, or bird) with the most poisonous part of their bodies. Tail lashing and head butting are used by some species (certain newts and mole salamanders), and some Asian and European salamanders spray tiny jets of poison at their enemies. The Chinese spiny newt has sharp rib ends adjacent to poison glands in the skin. A predator attempting to bite the newt may be jabbed with the rib tips and poisoned with the toxic skin secretions.

In Michigan, salamanders in the genus *Ambystoma* (blue-spotted, spotted, tiger, and small-mouthed salamanders) occasionally display tail-lashing behavior and probably have slightly toxic skin secretions. The eastern newt, particularly the eft stage, is quite distasteful to many predators. The red phase of the red-backed salamander may mimic the color of the more noxious red eft, perhaps giving some protection to this otherwise defenseless animal. Although it is generally safe to handle Michigan salamanders, avoid getting amphibian skin secretions in your mouth, nose, or eyes. Conversely, amphibians can be harmed by insect repellents, certain skin care products, solvents, and other chemicals. They should be handled only with clean hands, if at all!

Salamanders cannot regulate their body temperatures internally and are quickly killed by extreme temperatures or dryness. Terrestrial species avoid freezing, overheating, and desiccation by remaining buried in the soil or beneath logs and leaf litter. Some Michigan salamanders may be active at rather low temperatures. For instance, the spotted salamander will move to breeding ponds at air temperatures only slightly above freezing, while mudpuppies are often seen swimming below the ice in winter.

FOOD AND FEEDING

Both adult and larval salamanders are carnivorous, generally feeding on small invertebrates such as earthworms, snails, crustaceans, mites, and insects. Larger larvae may also feed on smaller siblings or the larvae of other species. Although sirens have been found with large amounts of plant material in their digestive tracts, it is likely that they swallowed the plants while feeding on small aquatic animals.

Most salamanders actively hunt for their food, unlike frogs and toads which usually sit and wait for their prey. Salamanders use both sight and smell to locate food, and smell is undoubtedly important for burrowing species that live underground. Aquatic newts reportedly locate pill clams, a favorite food, by scent alone.

Methods of catching food can vary from species to species. Aquatic salamanders can suck in prey by suddenly opening their mouths and expanding their throats. Mole salamanders have a short, thick tongue attached to the front of the mouth which can be flipped out to capture prey. Red-backed salamanders have a long, sticky tongue that can shoot out at prey animals.

Breeding pond used by blue-spotted salamanders.

SALAMANDER REPRODUCTION

Salamander reproductive habits are more difficult to observe than those of frogs and toads. Being largely silent creatures, they do not announce their breeding activities with their voices, and many Michigan species complete their courtship and egg laying in the earliest days of spring, often with ice and snow still around woodland ponds.

In pond breeding species, such as spotted and tiger salamanders, a courting male rubs and nudges the female with his snout and eventually tries to get her to follow him. She may nudge the male's tail and cloaca as she follows, and the pair may even go in circles for some time. The male eventually deposits a blob of jelly-like material capped with sperm (called a spermatophore) which the female then picks up with her cloaca. Although courtship takes place in water, fertilization is internal, since the sperm fuse with the eggs within the female salamander's body.

J. A. Fowler

Spermatophore of the blue-spotted salamander.

In blue-spotted salamanders and newts, courting males may clasp females with their limbs, a behavior similar to amplexus in frogs. Unlike frogs, however, salamanders do not lay eggs during this clasping phase.

Most Michigan salamanders deposit their eggs underwater in gelatinous masses, and the eggs hatch into aquatic larvae with external gills. The larvae usually lose their gills and transform into the adult form in late summer or fall. The two species of permanently aquatic salamanders, the mudpuppy and the lesser siren, retain their gills as adults, and tiger salamanders sometimes become mature and breed in the aquatic gilled form.

Marbled salamander eggs.

Three Michigan species deposit eggs on land. The marbled salamander lays its eggs in low areas that will be flooded by fall rains. The eggs then hatch into typical pond-type larvae. The red-backed salamander deposits its eggs underground or in a cavity within a rotted log. The gilled larval stage is passed within the egg, and the salamanders hatch as tiny replicas of the adults. The four-toed salamander lays eggs in moss overhanging the water, into which the larvae fall after hatching.

Newts have a different life cycle than other Michigan salamanders. Their eggs hatch into gilled larvae which develop into a nonbreeding, land-living form called the eft. After two or more years on land, the eft returns to the water as an aquatic breeding adult without gills.

CONSERVATION OF FROGS, TOADS, AND SALAMANDERS

Frogs and toads enjoy a good reputation with humans. Their springtime choruses are a pleasure to hear and a symbol of winter's end. Most people enjoy seeing them, whether in wetlands or suburban gardens.

Adult frogs and toads feed mostly on insects, some of which are pests to humans. Many gardeners and agriculturalists recognize the benefits of frog and toad populations. It is estimated that a single Blanchard's cricket frog —an increasingly rare species in Michigan— could eat about 4,800 insects in a year. A hundred cricket frogs would thus eat about 480,000 insects, and a thousand frogs perhaps 4.8 million insects. Clearly, the loss of these tiny frogs from a wetland could have a significant impact on the ecosystem.

Larger frogs eat larger prey animals, and green frogs and bullfrogs might occasionally feed on species valued by humans, such as fish and smaller frogs. However, their impact on game species is undoubtedly minor, and large frogs are themselves valued as the source of frog legs used for human food. To prevent their overharvest, the Michigan Department of Natural Resources regulates the harvest of frogs through closed seasons and bag limits. **Always check**

with the Department of Natural Resources for current regulations before capturing frogs for any reason.

Despite their shy and inconspicuous nature, salamanders are important animals in the ecosystem, acting as predators on insects and other small animals. A study of an 89-acre woodland in New Hampshire found that salamanders outnumbered the birds and mammals combined and that the combined living weight of salamanders was more than two and one-half times that of birds at the peak of the nesting season. This woods was similar to those found in Michigan, and 93.5 percent of the salamanders found there were red-backed salamanders,

Red-Backed Salamander.

a species abundant in Michigan. It is clear that these little amphibians can be at least as important in a forest ecosystem as the birds and mammals, and their loss would be equally disastrous. Adult and larval salamanders are sometimes captured for fish bait or for the pet trade. To prevent their overharvest, the Michigan Department of Natural Resources regulates their taking through closed seasons and bag limits. As with frogs, **always check current regulations before capturing salamanders.**

Many biologists and naturalists are concerned about the growing number of frog, toad, and salamander species that are becoming rare or even disappearing. While some of these troubled species live in tropical environments, many others are temperate species, and some live in Michigan. The tiny Blanchard's cricket frog has declined or even disappeared from many places where it was once common and is now listed as a "species

Ponds and wetlands are critical habitats for amphibians.

of special concern" by the Michigan Department of Natural Resources. The marbled and small-mouthed salamanders are protected under the Michigan Endangered Species Act because of their scarcity in the state.

While some amphibians have small ranges in Michigan, it is not only peripheral species that have problems. The northern leopard frog was once the most conspicuous and perhaps the most common frog in the state. Beginning in the late 1960s, numbers of leopard frogs began to decline in many parts of Michigan (and other parts of its range as well), and by the mid-1970s they had all but disappeared from some areas.

Leopard frogs practically disappeared from parts of Michigan in the 1970s.

Though some local recovery has occurred in recent years, leopard frogs are still a long way from regaining their former abundance.

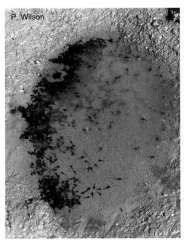
Toad tadpoles in a drying pond.

Biologists are trying to learn why some amphibians are declining, but the answers are often hard to find. Habitat loss and degradation are certainly primary problems. Over half of the estimated original 11 million acres of wetland habitats in Michigan have been destroyed by human activities, and those remaining are often subjected to various pollutants or other forms of misuse. Since nearly all of Michigan's frogs, toads, and salamanders depend on wetlands during part or all of their lives, the loss of this habitat has taken its toll. However, laws protecting wetlands that recently have been passed at the state and local level should help save some habitat.

Amphibians may offer ecologists an early warning of environmental problems because of their biological traits and varied habitat requirements. Most frogs, toads, and salamanders live in different habitats at different times in their lives. Many species breed in ponds, lakes, or marshes but live in woodlands as adults. Newly transformed leopard frogs leave the water and often disperse widely through marshes and upland meadows and even suburban yards. In addition, amphibians have thin, permeable skins through which water (and many chemicals carried in water) can easily pass. We already know that some amphibian species are very sensitive to the effects of acid rain and have practically disappeared from parts of the United States where bodies of water are greatly acidified.

Although habitat loss and pollution are the most serious threats to our amphibians, there are others. Many thousands of frogs and salamanders are killed on roads every year. In some places roads were built through traditional migration routes, often between uplands where adult salamanders or frogs live and the wetlands where they breed. In some areas large numbers of frogs and salamanders have been collected for the biological supply trade to be used as research animals, dissected in science classes, or sold as pets. In some parts of the country, small frogs and larval salamanders are popular fish bait. The harvest of larger frogs for frog legs, particularly when done on a commercial basis, can be a significant drain on their populations.

Frogs, toads, and salamanders have always suffered a high rate of loss to natural predators such as fish, birds, snakes, and mammals. In fact, a major role of amphibians in the ecosystem is providing food for other animals, and their reproductive abilities are geared towards having large numbers of young to balance the losses. But when humans enter the picture, many amphibian species may not be able to withstand additional pressures.

There are many things you can do to assure that frogs, toads, and salamanders survive as a part of our wildlife heritage:

✔ Support state and local efforts to preserve wetlands and adjacent natural habitats, and preserve habitats on your own property.

✔ Find alternatives to building new roads in or near wetlands.

✔ Where local wetlands are scarce or have been eliminated, construct ponds or remove old drain tiles or drainage ditches to restore amphibian breeding habitat. (Note: Always obey local and state regulations when digging in or modifying wetlands, and be sensitive to effects on adjacent property owners.)

✔ Resist stocking ponds with game fish that eat tadpoles and salamander larvae. Or construct two ponds—one for fishing and one for other wildlife.

✔ Avoid using pesticides, fertilizers, and potentially toxic substances in and around amphibian habitats.

✔ Don't use amphibians as fish bait, and discourage the large-scale use of wild-caught amphibians as laboratory and educational subjects. There are usually good alternatives to using amphibians for these purposes. While collecting small numbers of common species for personal use may not seem to be a serious problem, collecting large numbers of any species can seriously damage the affected population.

STUDYING FROGS, TOADS, AND SALAMANDERS

The best way to study frogs, toads, and salamanders is to observe them in their natural habitats. Frog or salamander watching is like bird watching — you must go to the right place at the right time to find them.

Frogs are most easily found during their breeding season when their calls tell you where and what kinds of frogs they are. A good way to observe frogs is to go out on a rainy night with a flashlight. Many species sit still and even continue singing while in a flashlight beam. With practice, you can learn to identify the different calls, perhaps using the recordings listed in the bibliography. Even after the breeding season, frogs are not hard to find. Some species, such as green and bullfrogs, stay near pond and lake edges, while others move into new habitats. You most likely will see wood frogs, spring peepers, and treefrogs in woodlands, while leopard frogs wander widely through meadows and grassy backyards.

Salamanders are also easier to observe during their breeding season. Finding breeding groups of the larger species, such as the blue-spotted, spotted, and tiger salamanders, usually means going out early in spring after the first snow-melting rains and searching woodland ponds at night with a flashlight. Use caution when wading and watch for deep spots. Be careful not to disturb the salamanders or their egg masses. After the breeding season, salamanders can be found by turning rotting logs, flat rocks, or other objects.

Always be kind to the habitat. Replace turned logs and try not to trample vegetation. Don't over-handle amphibians, as the warmth of your hand is stressful to them. Don't touch amphibians if you have insect repellent or other chemicals on your hands.

After studying frogs, toads, and salamanders in the wild, some people may wish to observe a specimen or two in captivity. Schools and nature centers often

Hand-held American toad.

use live amphibians in educational displays. Although some Michigan species are fairly easy to maintain in captivity for brief periods, consider these questions before capturing any amphibian:

✔ Is there a good reason to remove the animal from the wild?

✔ Is it legal? A few species are protected in Michigan, and others have seasons and possession limits. Check with the DNR for current regulations.

✔ Does the species you wish to keep need special care?

✔ Can you provide a healthy environment for the animal?

✔ When you release the specimen, can it be returned to its original habitat?

Breeding site for the wood frog.

GUIDELINES FOR CAPTIVE CARE

Recommended species: Large toads, frogs (green, leopard, and bullfrogs) and salamanders (tiger and spotted salamanders, newts, mudpuppies) are easiest to maintain. Most salamanders tend to stay out of sight and make poor display animals.

Not recommended: Small frogs (peepers, chorus frogs) and salamanders (red-backed, four-toed, and small specimens of larger species) are difficult to feed and are sensitive to handling. Pickerel frogs can poison fellow tank-mates.

CARE OF ADULT AMPHIBIANS

Housing: A glass aquarium or clear plastic box can be turned into a terrarium for salamanders, wood frogs, tree frogs, and toads. Add three or four inches of soil, some plants (leave in pots for easy maintenance), and pieces of flat bark for hiding spots. Place a shallow water dish so that specimens can get in and out easily. Keep large frogs in simpler quarters where specimens can choose between being in or out of the water. Cover the bottom of the tank with smooth pea gravel or a similar substance for drainage, and include a large, two- to three-inch-deep water dish that specimens can enter or leave easily. A tank filled directly with a few inches of water, with a large sloping rock as a land area, is also suitable but harder to clean. Allow for ventilation, but always keep the tank or terrarium covered to prevent escapes and to help hold in humidity.

Cleanliness is important in any amphibian display. A buildup of animal waste products can cause specimens to become sick and die. Terraria must be cleaned and soil replaced regularly. Larger animals require more frequent cleaning. Never use soap or cleaning solvents.

It is important to keep numbers of specimens low. Overcrowding can lead to disease. A terrarium in a ten-gallon tank might be sufficient for one or two toads or wood frogs, but large frogs need more space per specimen.

Tanks for aquatic specimens such as mudpuppies and newts can be set up as you would for fish. Keep the water level an inch or two below the rim. It is wise to use some kind of aeration or filtration system (available in tropical fish stores) to keep the water clean. Aquatic plants provide hiding places for the animals and give the tank a natural look. If your water supply is chlorinated, hold the water in an open bucket for a day or two before using it. Replacing a portion of the water every few days prevents a buildup of waste products in the tank.

Light and heat: Frogs, toads, and salamanders do not usually need extra lighting beyond that found in most rooms. If artificial lighting is desired, use a low-heat fluorescent light. Some amphibians may benefit from the use of wide-spectrum fluorescent tubes that give off a light similar to sunlight. Never expose a terrarium or aquarium to direct sunlight, as it can quickly overheat.

Native frogs and salamanders normally do well at room temperature (about 65°-75°F). Large frogs can tolerate warmer temperatures, but many species are stressed at temperatures above 80°F. On hot summer days, amphibians in nature burrow deep into moist soil or move to cool waters. When caring for captive amphibians during hot weather, it may be necessary to move them to a cool basement or an air-conditioned room.

Feeding: All adult frogs, toads, and salamanders are carnivores that eat live insects, worms, and other small creatures. Some large frogs eat smaller frogs, so it is best to segregate specimens by size.

Earthworms are a favorite food of salamanders and toads. Make sure that you obtain these from places free of pesticide residues. In captivity, large salamanders often learn to take strips of lean beef or liver wiggled in front of them. If such foods are used frequently, it is best to dust a powdered pet·vitamin/mineral supplement on each item to provide a proper nutrient balance.

Offer frogs and toads a variety of live insects, but avoid feeding ants and houseflies. You can catch insects by sweeping an insect net through fields or grassy places, or you can buy crickets and mealworms (flour beetle larvae) from some pet shops. If captive-raised insects

Tiger salamander larva eating a worm.

are used often, lightly dust them with powdered vitamin supplement before feeding.

Note: Most frogs, toads, and salamanders will not recognize or take food unless it is moving, so live insects are required.

Aquatic species can be fed earthworms, tubifex worms, other small aquatic invertebrates, and small fish. Some specimens will take small bits of lean beef or liver, wiggled on a toothpick. Do not let water become foul with uneaten food.

The amount of food offered depends on the size and activity of the specimen. A small, active toad or treefrog may need to eat each day, while a large, sedentary salamander may require only one or two worms per week.

RAISING TADPOLES AND SALAMANDER LARVAE

Tadpoles and salamander larvae can be raised in an aquarium or almost any clean waterproof container. The tank can be set up as for fish, with aquatic plants to provide cover. Large tanks require aeration or filtration. Use chlorine-free or aged water. A primary rule is to keep the number of specimens small to avoid

Transforming gray treefrog.

overcrowding and cannibalism. Drain and replace a portion of the water every few days to prevent a buildup of waste products.

Tadpoles can be collected in spring in most ponds and wetlands. Teachers and naturalists wishing to demonstrate metamorphosis should remember that toad, wood frog, and treefrog tadpoles may transform in six weeks or less if kept in a warm environment, but the larger tadpoles of green frogs and bullfrogs may take more than one summer to become frogs.

Most tadpoles are omnivorous and feed on algae and other soft plant material and occasionally scavenge dead siblings and other organisms. In captivity, substitute boiled leaf lettuce and spinach and small amounts of flake fishfood if natural food is unavailable.

When the tadpoles develop legs and begin to look like frogs, provide a sloping rock or ramp in the tank. As their lungs develop, they must be able to leave the water or they will drown. The tiny froglets are very hard to feed and should be released in proper habitat soon after their tails are absorbed.

Salamander larvae are carnivorous. Small ones can be fed live brine shrimp or tubifex worms (available at tropical fish stores), or daphnia (a tiny crustacean common in shallow ponds). Larger specimens will eat small earthworms. As gills begin to shrink, provide a way for them to leave the water.

Health problems in captive amphibians are not common and can usually be traced to overcrowding, dirty or stagnant water, injuries from rough handling, or improper diet. If specimens refuse food or look unhealthy, return them to their habitats before the situation becomes more serious.

FOR MORE INFORMATION

The following publications are recommended to readers seeking additional information on frogs, toads, and salamanders of the Great Lakes area and on amphibians in general.

Behler, J.L., and F.W. King. 1979. *The Audubon Society Field Guide to North American Reptiles and Amphibians.* New York: Alfred A. Knopf, Inc. 719 pp.

Conant, R., and J.T. Collins. 1991. *A Field Guide to Reptiles and Amphibians: Eastern and Central North America.* 3rd Ed. Boston: Houghton Mifflin Co. 450 pp.

Duellman, W.E., and L. Trueb. 1986. *Biology of Amphibians.* New York: McGraw-Hill, Inc. 670 pp.

Halliday, T.R., and K. Adler (Eds.) 1986. *The Encyclopedia of Reptiles and Amphibians.* New York: Facts On File, Inc. 152 pp.

Minton, S.A. 1972. *Amphibians and Reptiles of Indiana.* Indianapolis: Indiana Academy of Science. Monograph No. 3. 346 pp.

Pfingsten, R.A., and F.L. Downs (Eds.) 1989. *Salamanders of Ohio.* Columbus: Bulletin of the Ohio Biological Survey. Vol. 7, No. 2. 315 pp.

Ruthven, A.G., C. Thompson, and H.T. Gaige. 1928. *The Herpetology of Michigan.* Ann Arbor: University Museums, The Univ. of Michigan Handbook Ser. No. 3. 229 pp.

Smith, P.W. 1961. *The Amphibians and Reptiles of Illinois.* Urbana: Bulletin of the Illinois Biological Survey. Vol. 28. 298 pp.

Tyning, T.F. 1990. *A Guide to Amphibians and Reptiles.* Boston: Little, Brown and Co. 400 pp.

Vogt, R.C. 1981. *Natural History of Amphibians and Reptiles of Wisconsin.* Milwaukee: Milwaukee Public Museum. 205 pp.

RECORDINGS OF FROG AND TOAD CALLS

Bogert, C.M. *Sounds of North American Frogs: The Biological Significance of Voice in Frogs.* New York: Folkways Records. Distributed by Rounder Records, Cambridge, Massachusetts, and Smithsonian Folkways Records, Rockville, Maryland. (Ninety-two calls of 50 species, with informative booklet.)

Kellogg, P.P., and A.A. Allen. *Voices of the Night. Sounds of Nature Series.* Boston: Houghton Mifflin (for Cornell Laboratory of Ornithology). (Calls of 34 species of frogs and toads of eastern North America.)

Eastern American toad calling.